ANIMALS OF THE SEA COLORING BOOK

Carlo Atzei

© 2020 Carlo Atzei. All rights reserved.

For enquiries, please contact **carloatzeicoloringbooks@gmail.com**

For information on future projects and other books, please follow the author's page on Amazon **amazon.com/author/carloatzei**
or the Instagram page **instagram.com/carloatzeiillustration/**

To receive exclusive content and updates, please subscribe to the newsletter by sending an email to **carloatzeicoloringbooks@gmail.com**

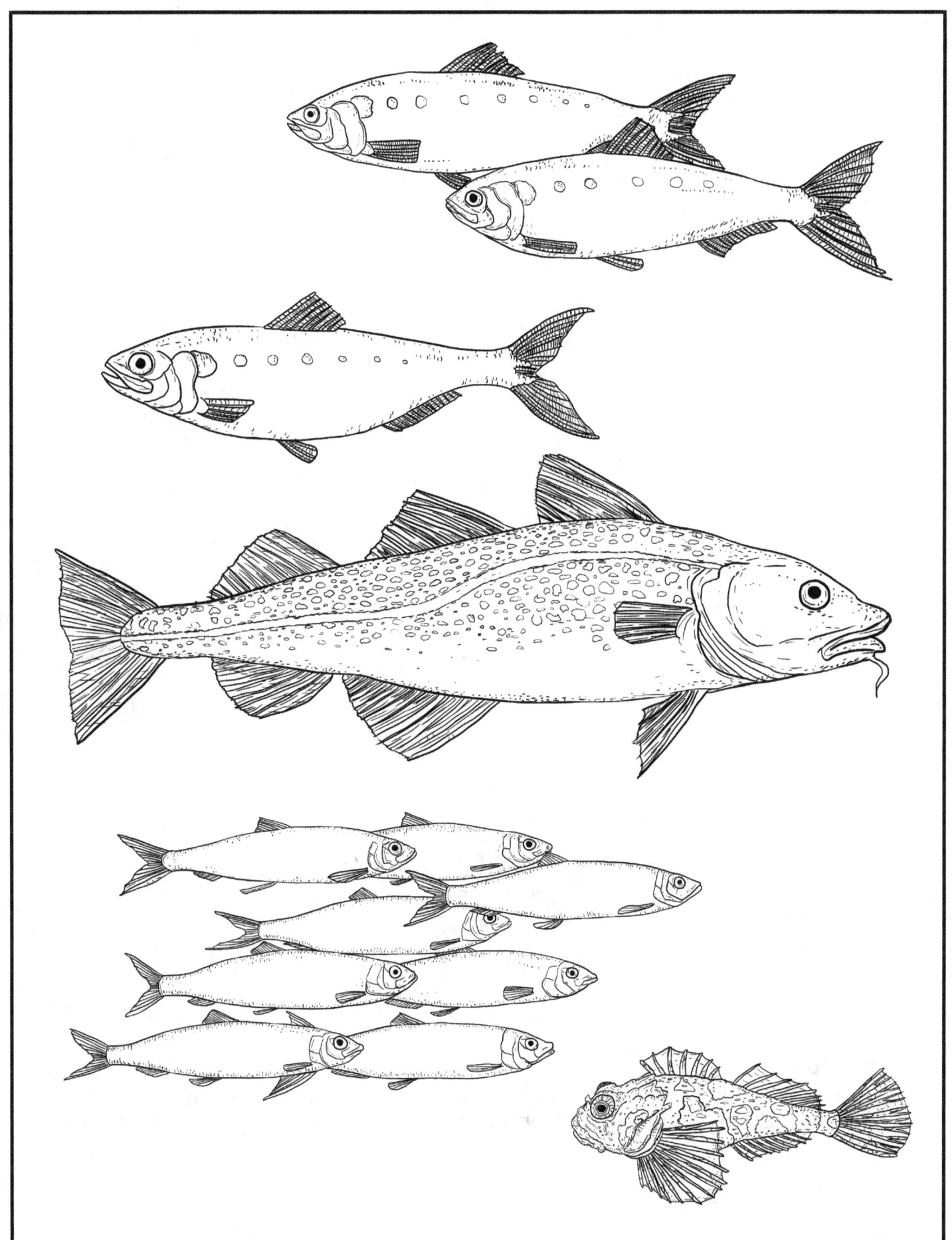

1. Baltic Sea
Animal species: twaite shad (Alosa fallax), Atlantic cod (Gadus morhua), Baltic herring (Clupea harengus membras), longspined bullhead (Taurulus bubalis)

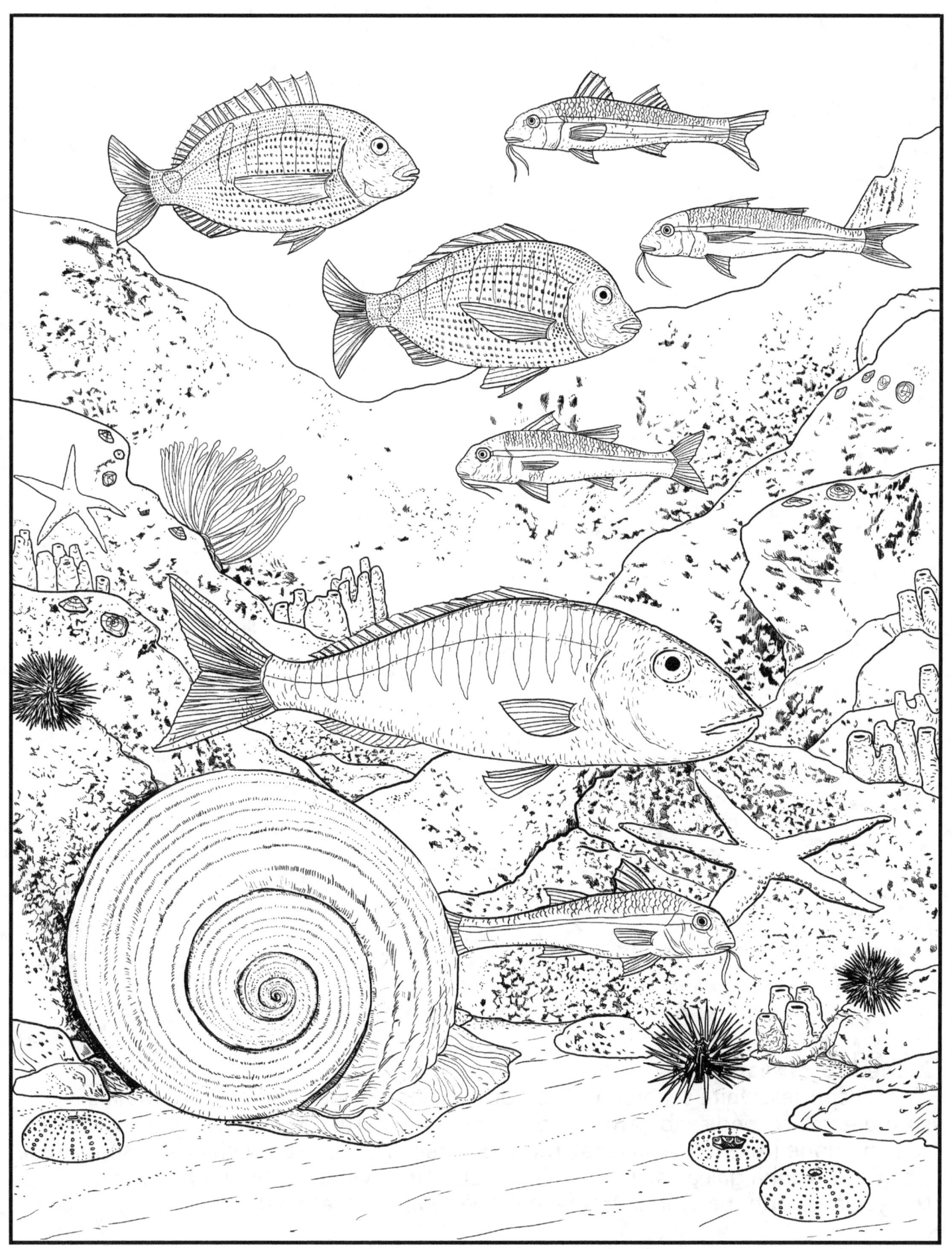

2. Mediterranean Sea
Animal species: white seabream (Diplodus sargus), striped red mullet (Mullus surmuletus), striped seabream (Lithognathus mormyrus), Mediterranean snakelocks sea anemone (Anemonia sulcata), Mediterranean red sea star (Echinaster sepositus), giant tun (Tonna galea), sea urchin (Paracentrotus lividus), yellow tube sponge (Aplysina aerophoba), Mediterranean limpet (Patella caerulea)

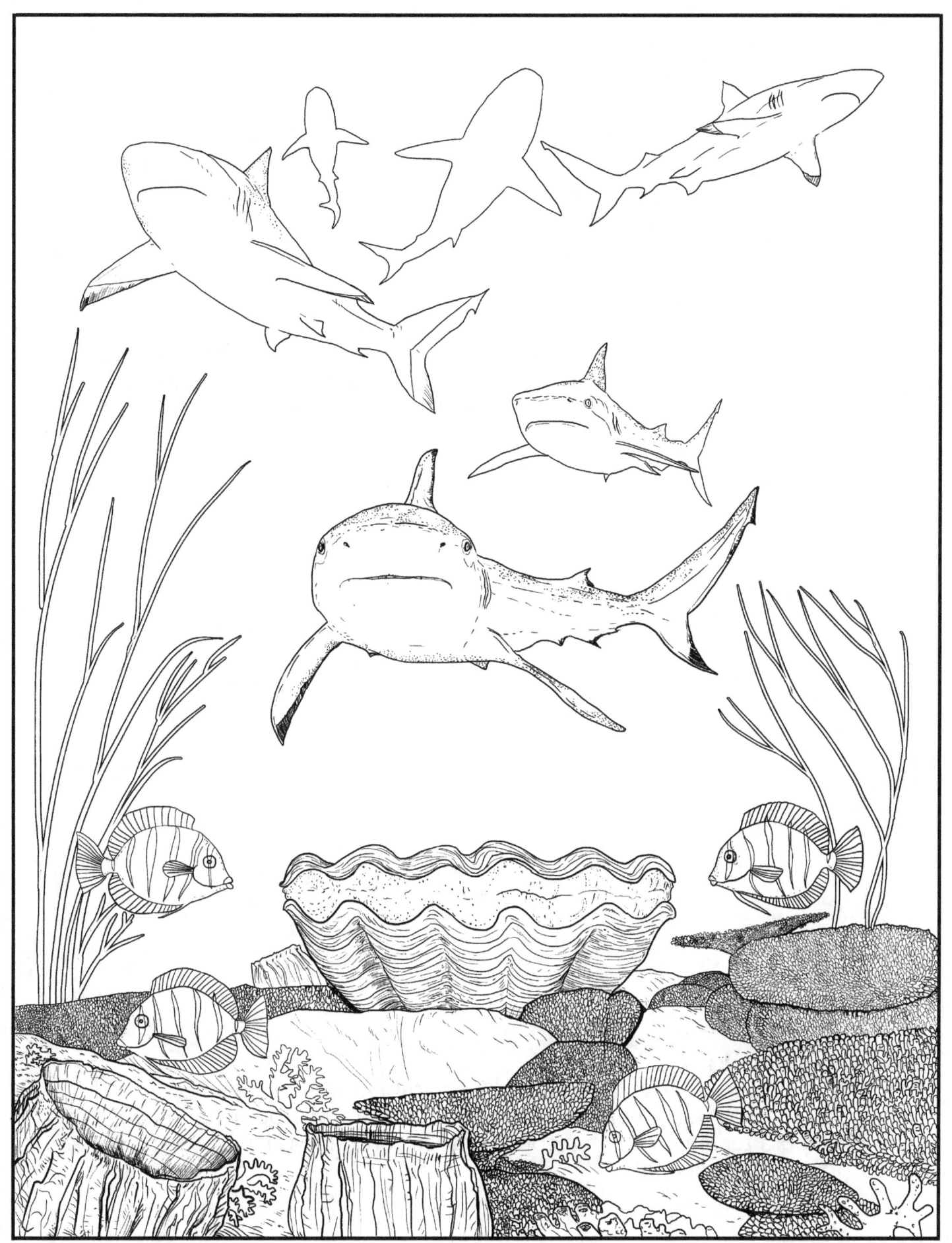

3. Grey Reef Sharks
Animal species: grey reef shark (Carcharhinus amblyrhynchos), giant clam (Tridacna gigas), convict tang (Acanthurus triostegus), table coral (Acropora cytherea), fire coral (Millepora tenera), red whip coral (Ellisella ceratophyta), barrel sponge (Xestospongia testudinaria)

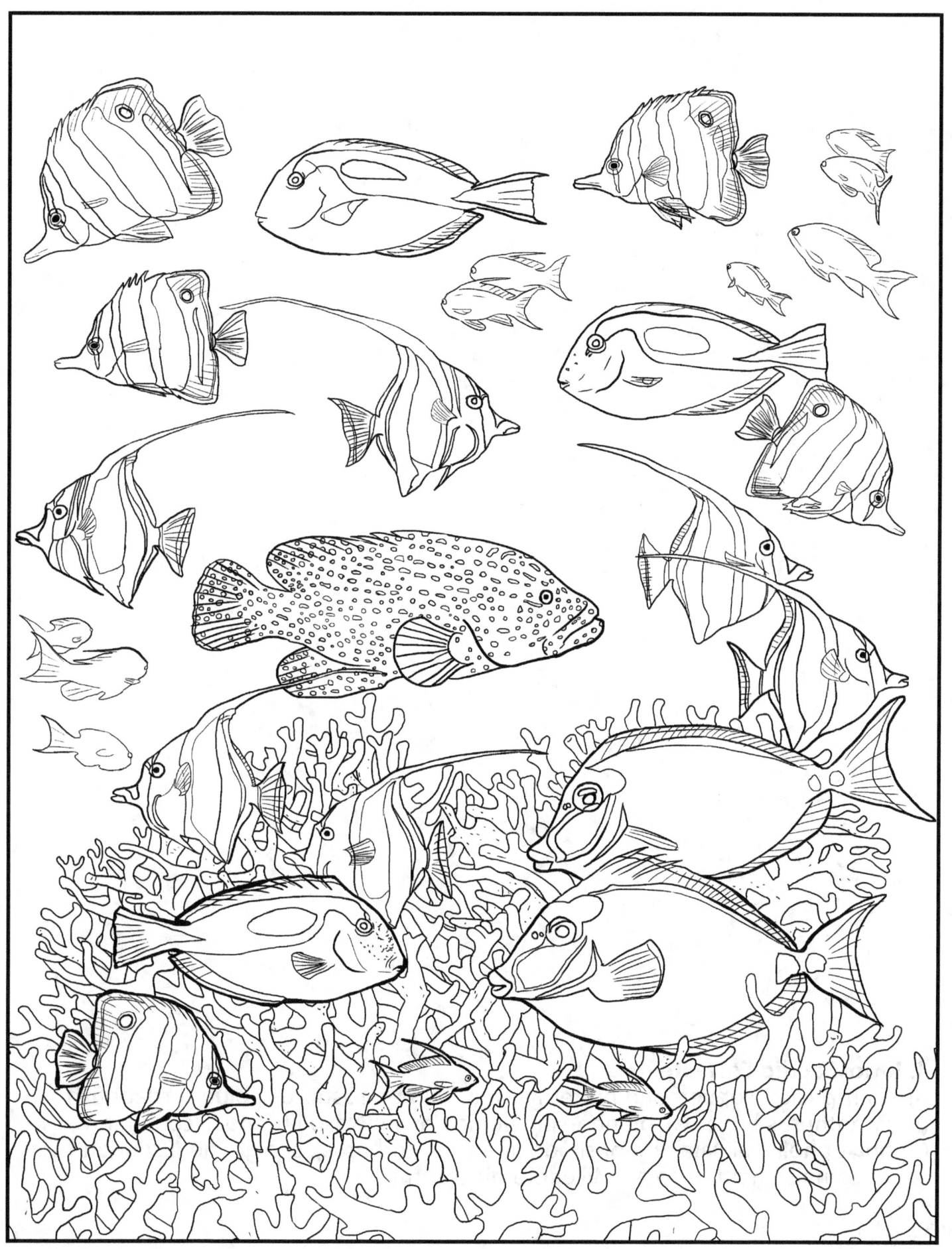

4. Indo-Pacific Coral Reef
Animal species: copperband butterflyfish (Chelmon rostratus), blue surgeonfish (Paracanthurus hepatus), orange-spine unicornfish (Naso lituratus), coral hind (Cephalopholis miniata), moorish idol (Zanclus cornutus), sea goldie (Pseudanthias squamipinnis), net fire coral (Millepora dichotoma)

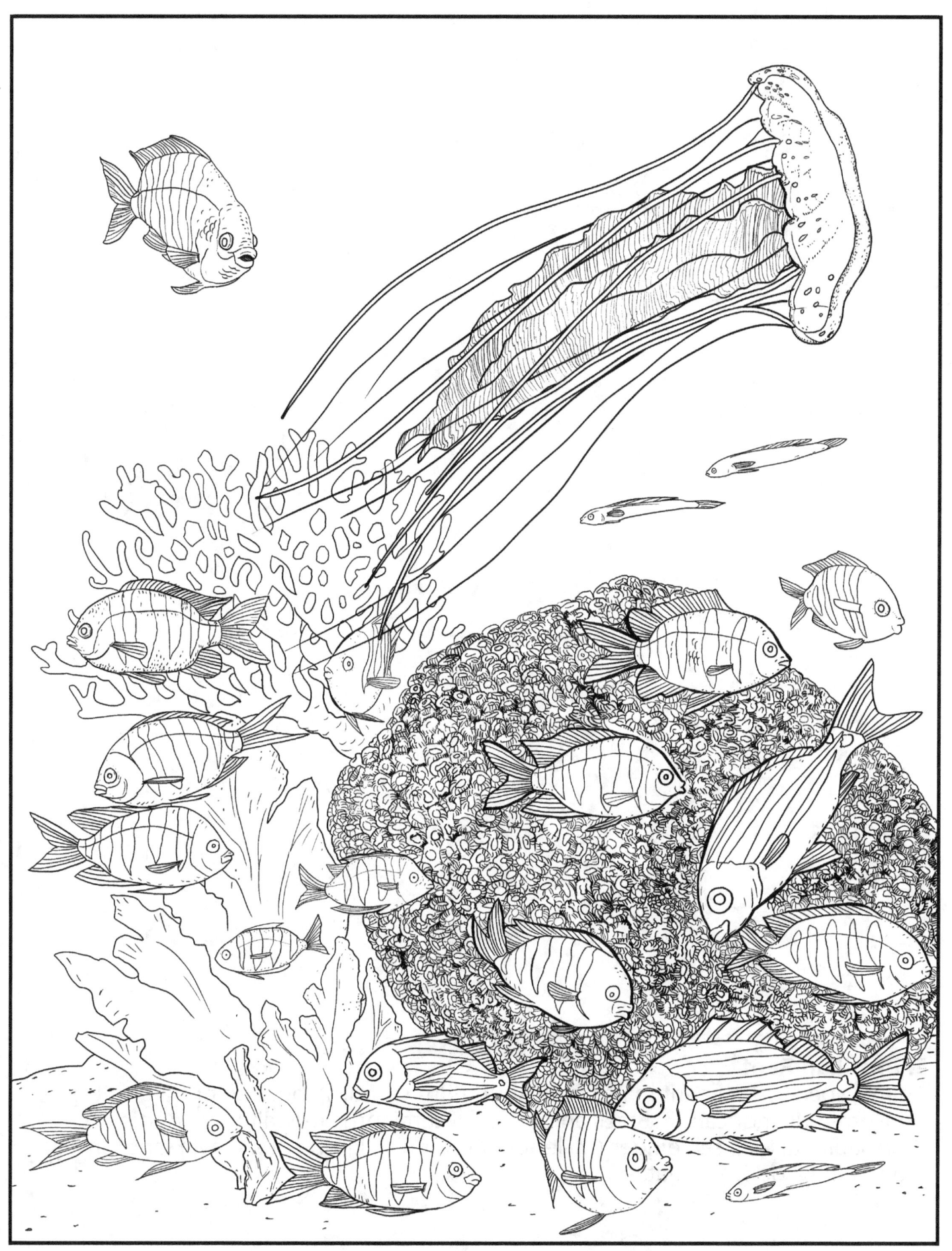

5. Brazilian Reef
Animal species: sergeant major fish (Abudefduf saxatilis), brownstriped grunt (Anisotremus moricandi), Brazilian dartfish (Ptereleotris randalli), sea nettle (Chrysaora lactea), sea ginger (Millepora alcicornis), knob coral (Favia leptophylla), sea fan (Phyllogorgia dilatata)

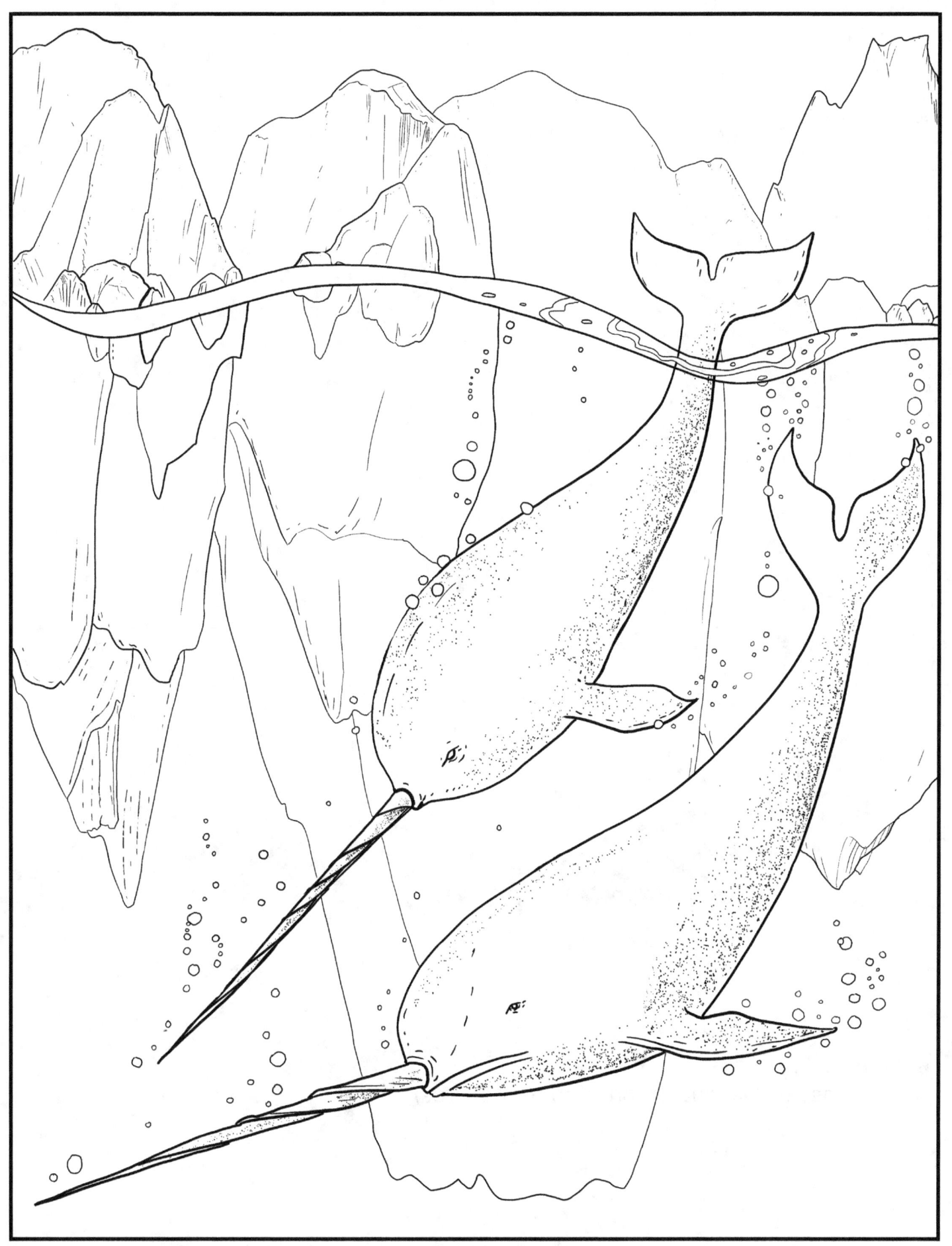

6. Narwhals
Animal species: narwhal (Monodon monoceros)

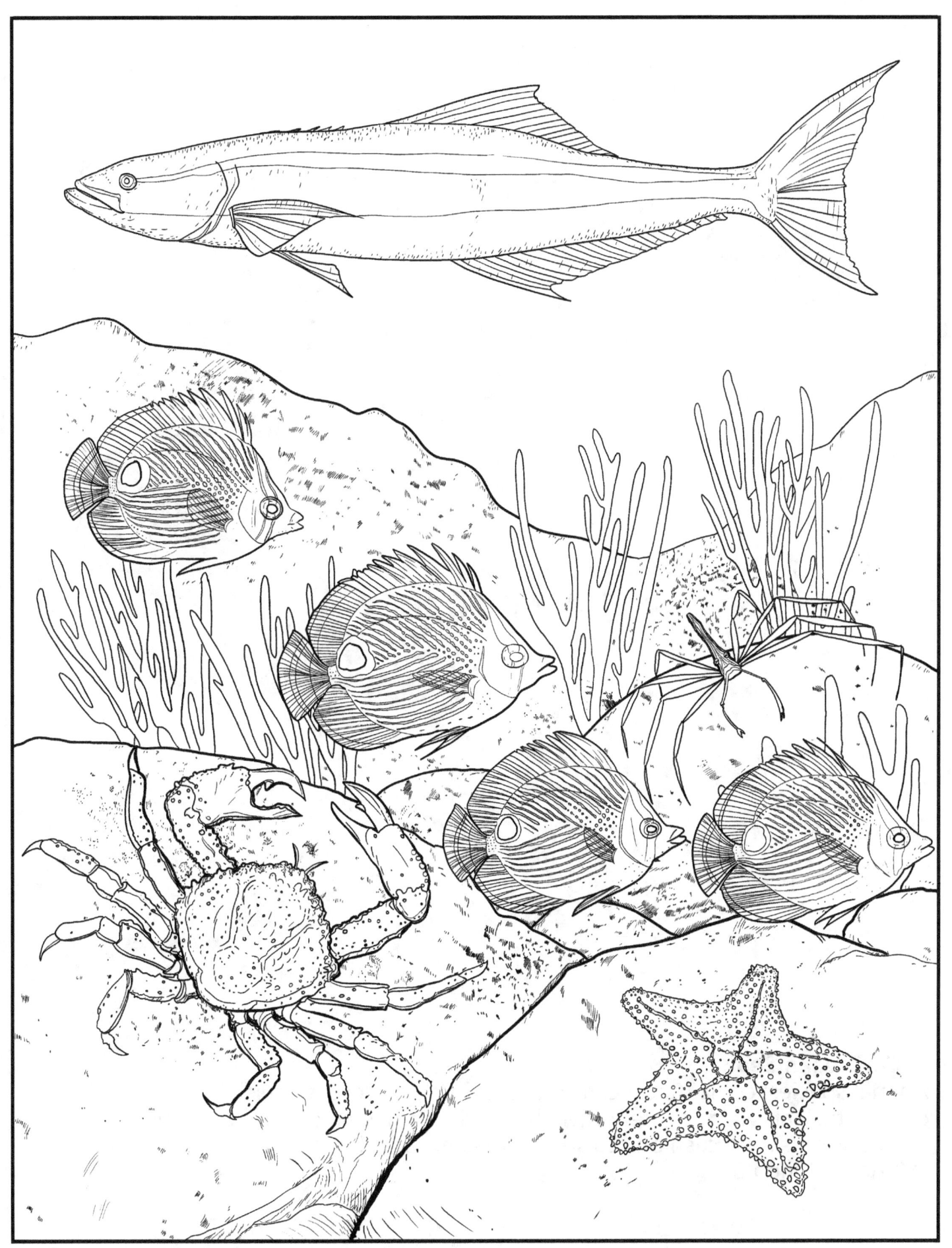

7. Caribbean Sea
Animal species: cobia (Rachycentron canadum), foureye butterflyfish (Chaetodon capistratus), arrow crab (Stenorhynchus seticornis), spiny spider crab (Mithrax spinosissimus), red cushion sea star (Oreaster reticulatus), orange spiny sea rod (Muricea elongata)

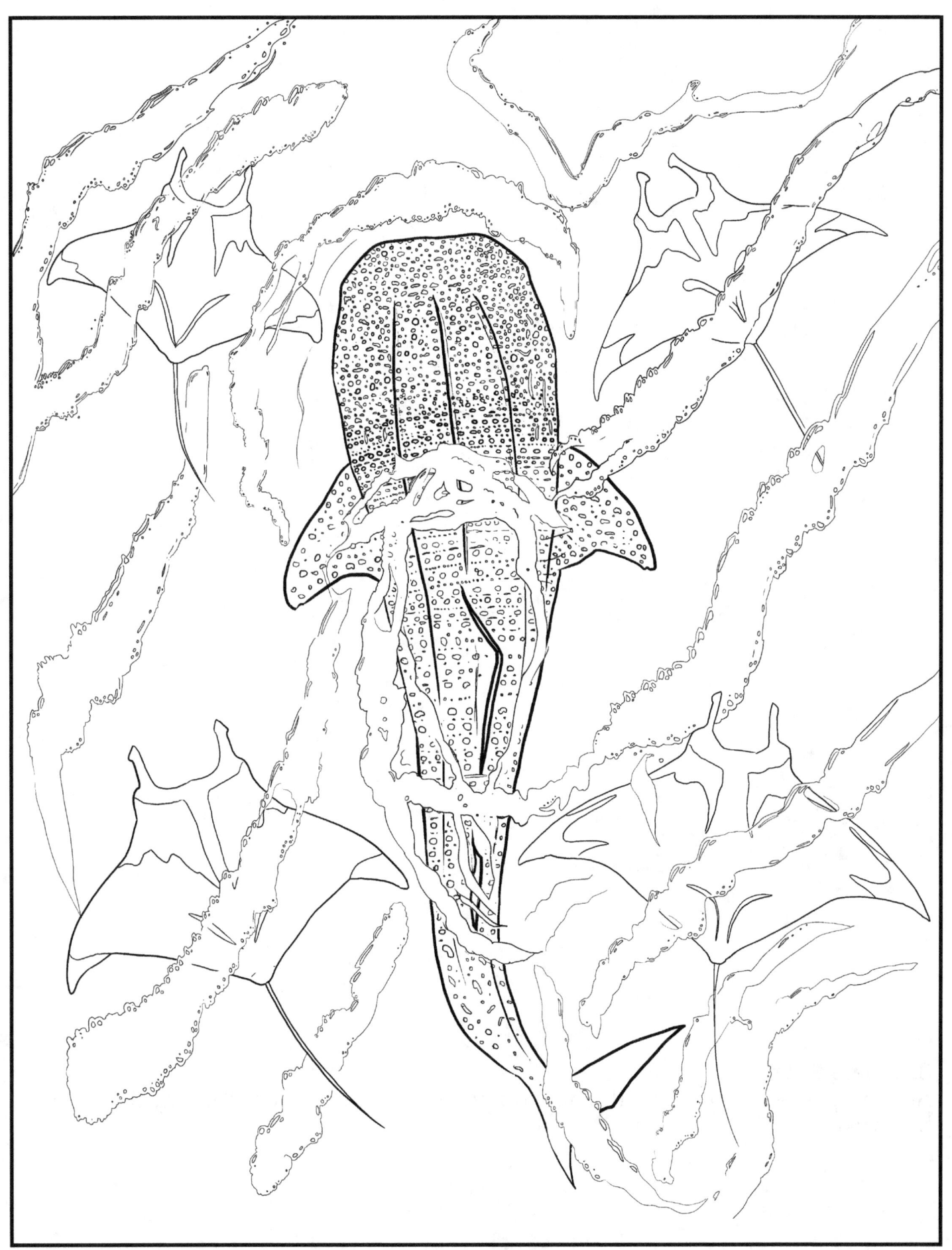

8. Whale Shark
Animal species: whale shark (Rhincodon typus), giant oceanic manta ray (Mobula birostris)

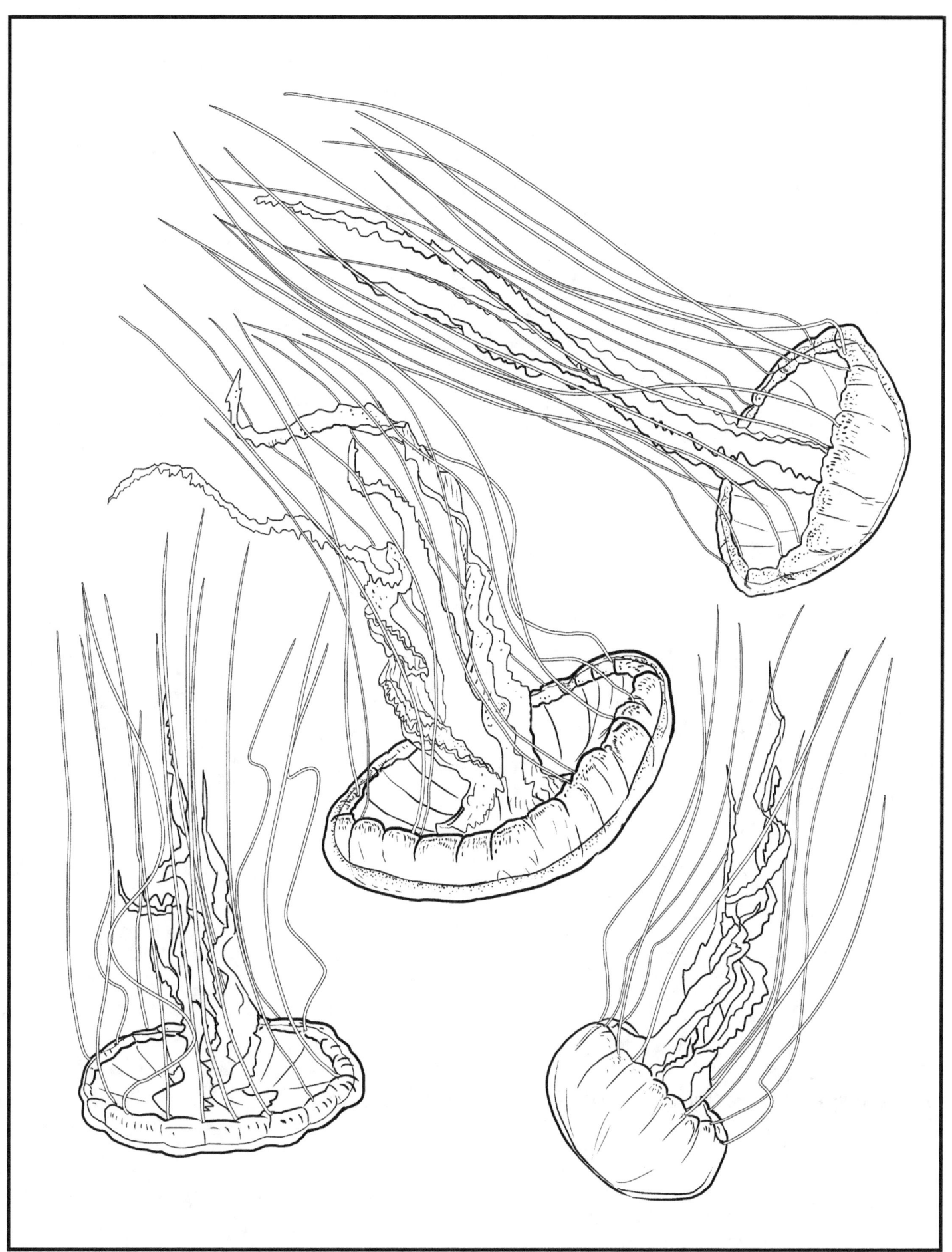

9. Sea Nettles
Animal species: Pacific sea nettle (Chrysaora fuscescens)

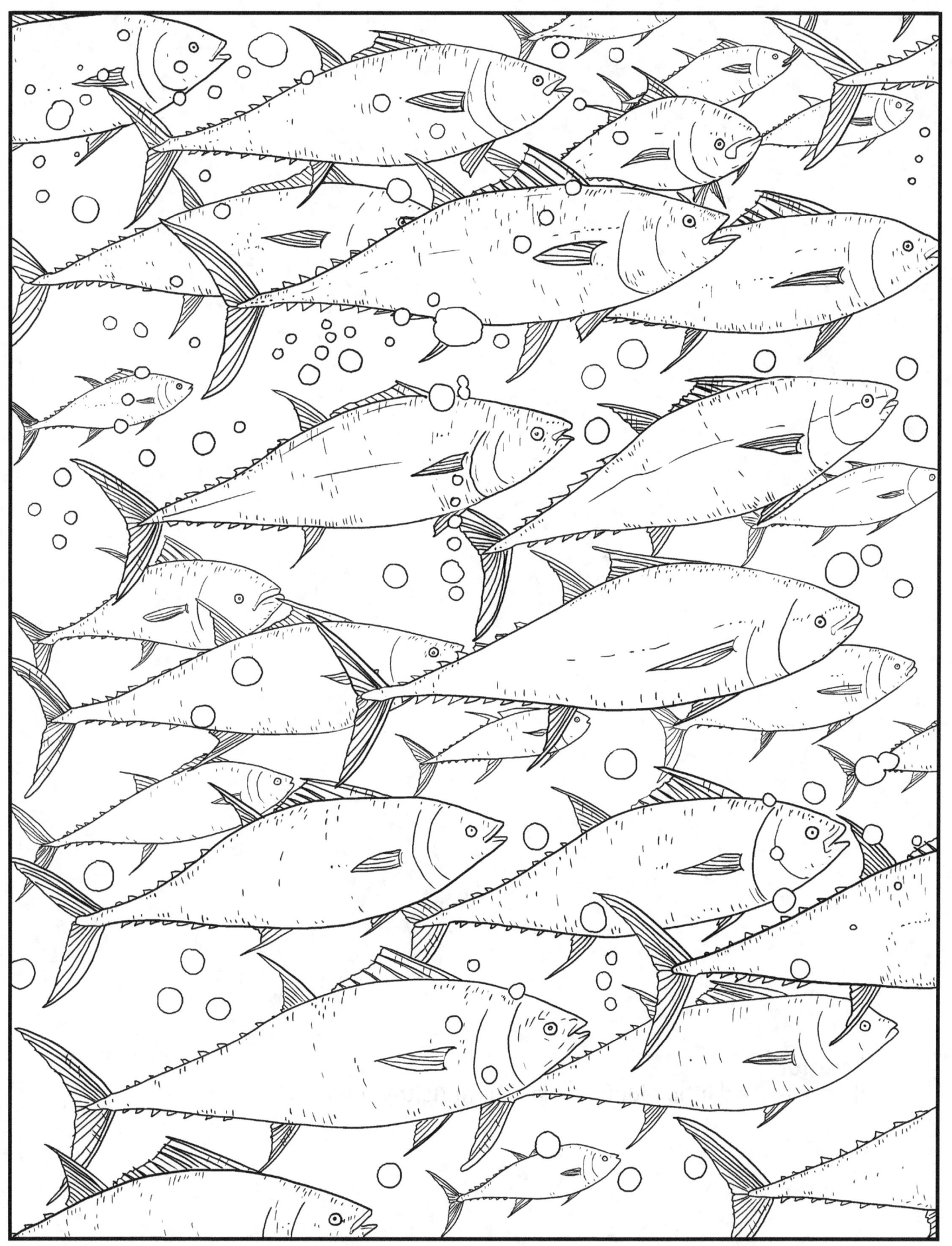

10. Migration
Animal species: Atlantic bluefin tuna (Thunnus thynnus)

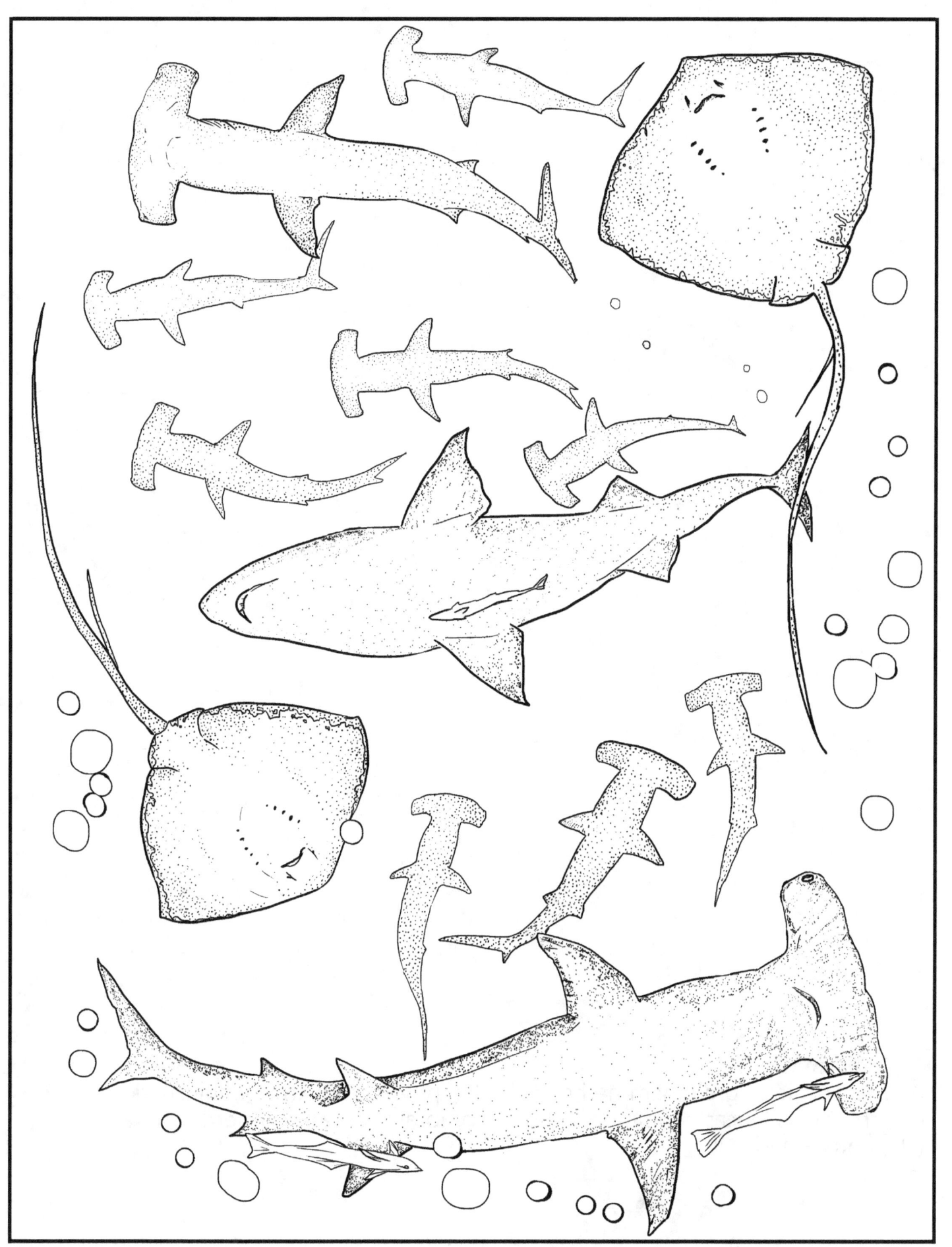

11. Bahamas
Animal species: great hammerhead shark (Sphyrna mokarran), bull shark (Carcharhinus leucas), common remora (Remora remora), southern stingray (Hypanus americanus)

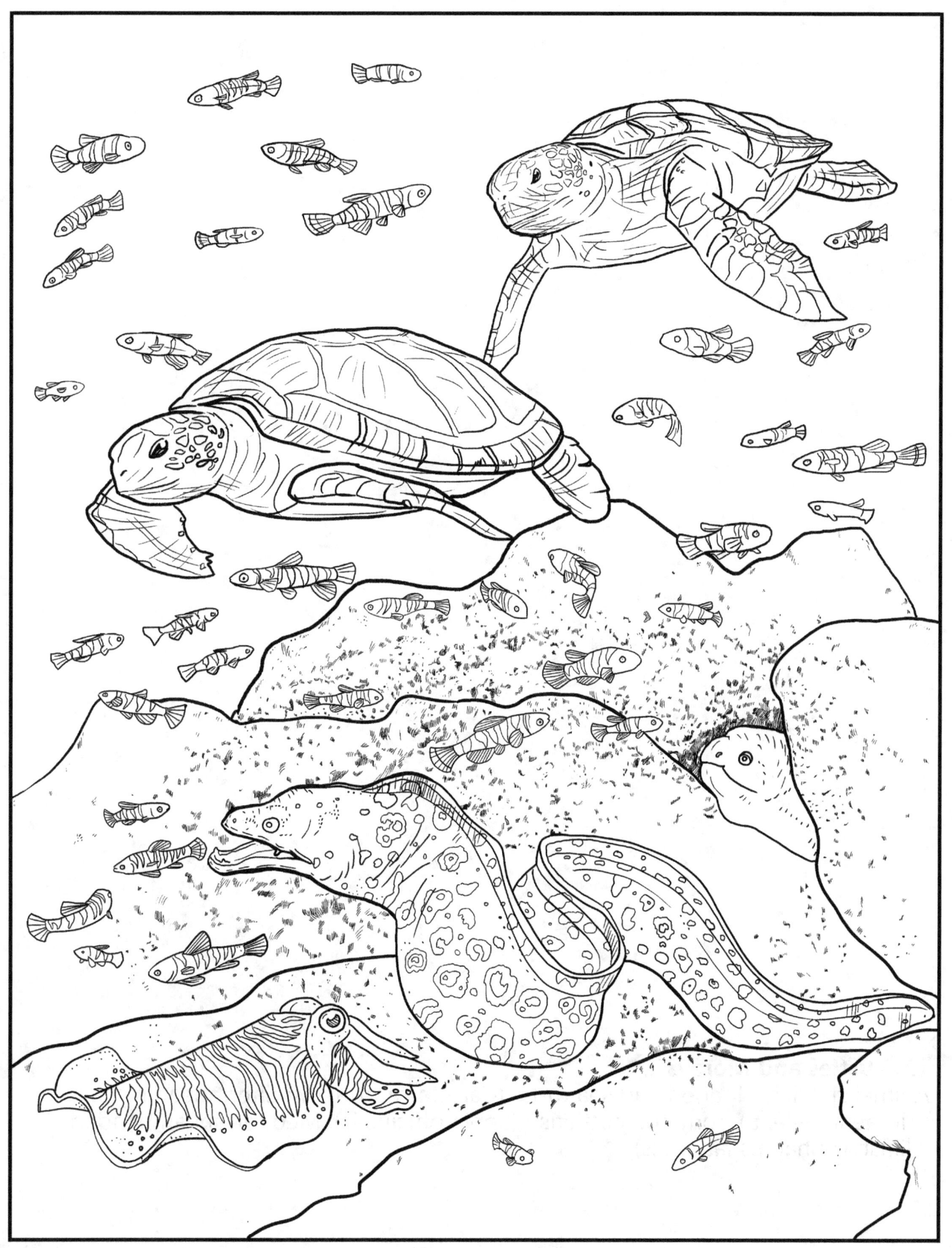

12. Turtles and Morays

Animal species: loggerhead sea turtle (Caretta caretta), Mediterranean moray (Muraena helena), common cuttlefish (Sepia officinalis), Mediterranean banded killifish (Aphanius fasciatus)

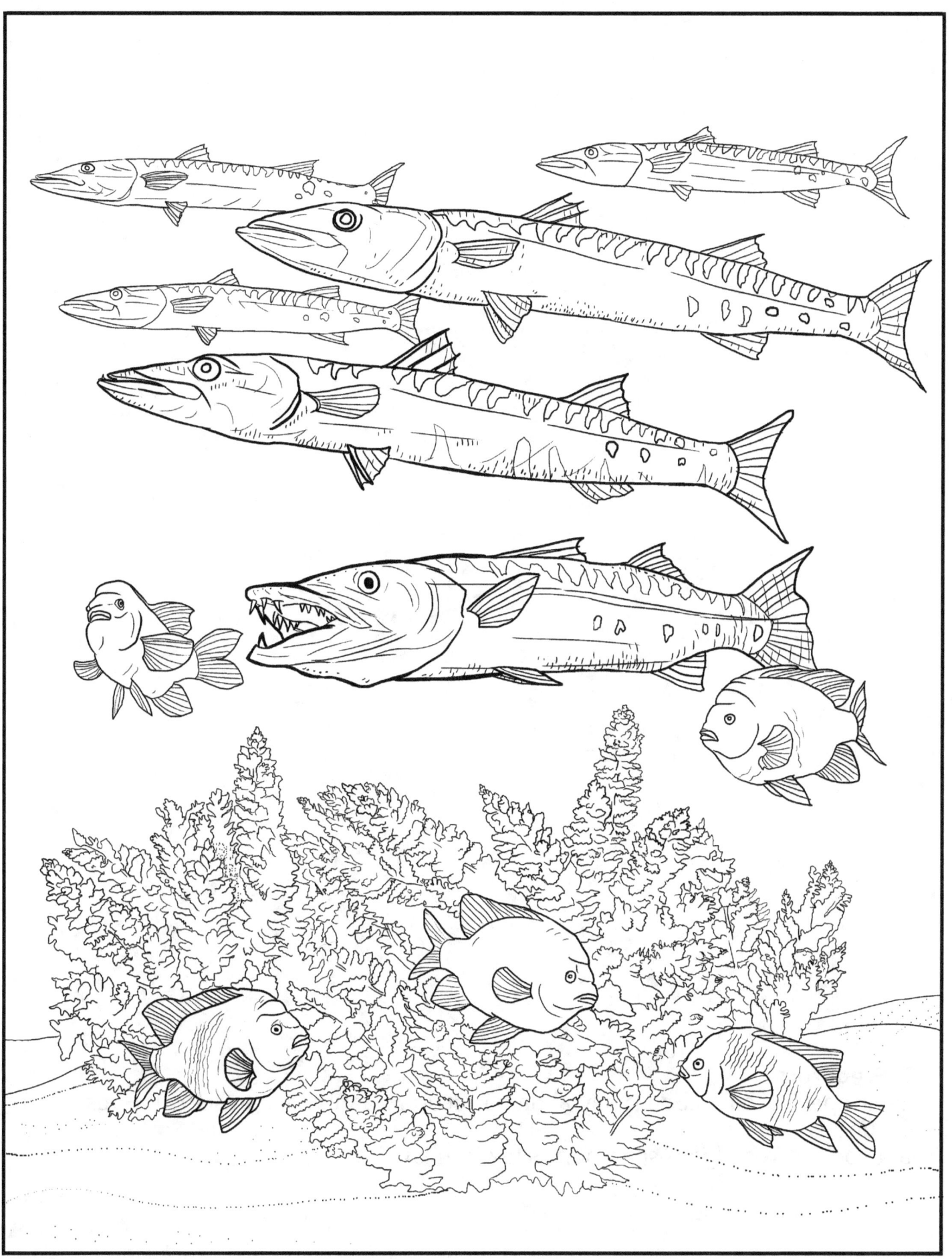

13. Predators
Animal species: barracuda (Sphyraena barracuda), Garibaldi damselfish (Hypsypops rubicundus)
Plant species: red alga (Asparagopsis taxiformis)

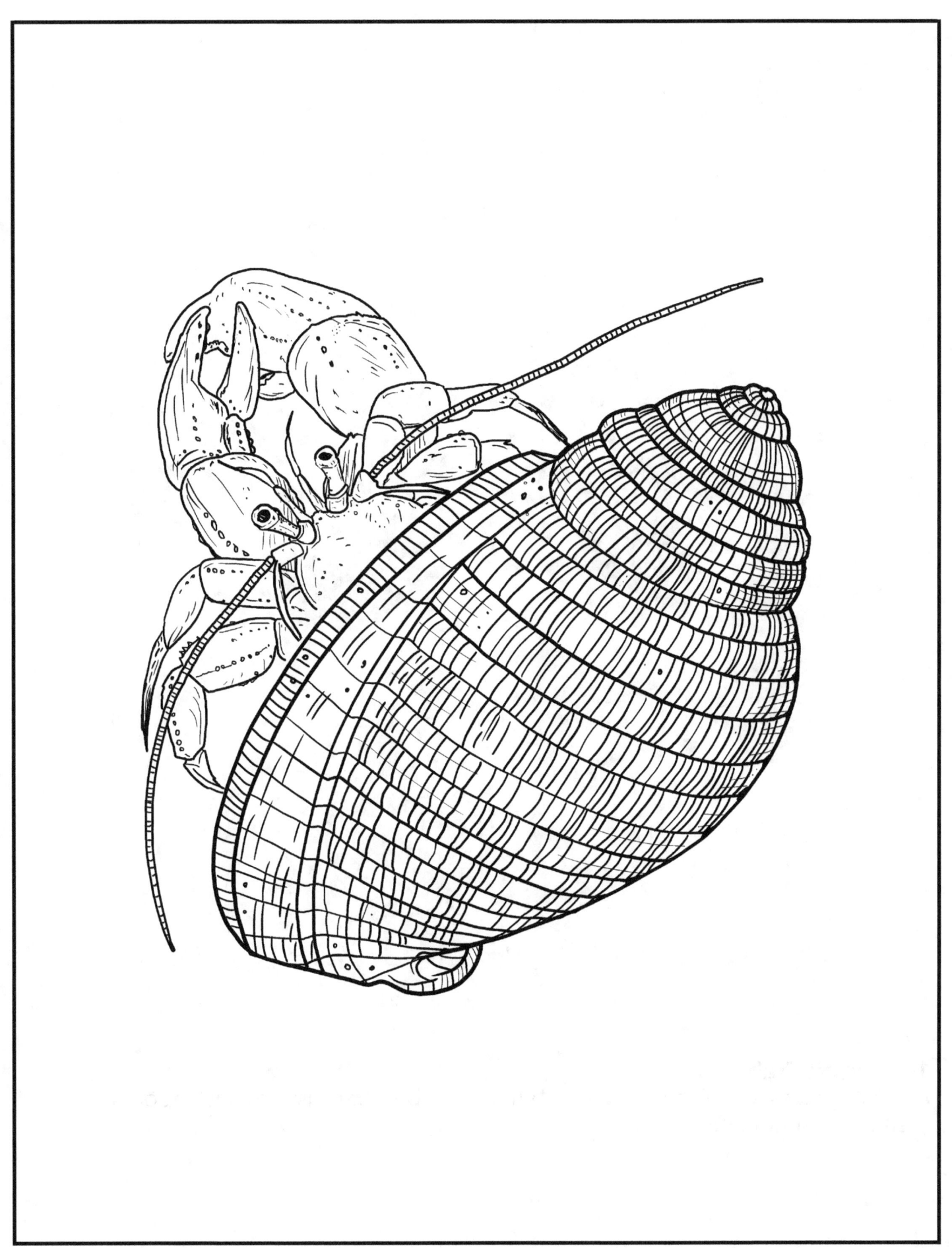

14. Hermit Crab
Animal species: common hermit crab (Pagurus bernhardus) in gastropod shell (Semicassis undulata)

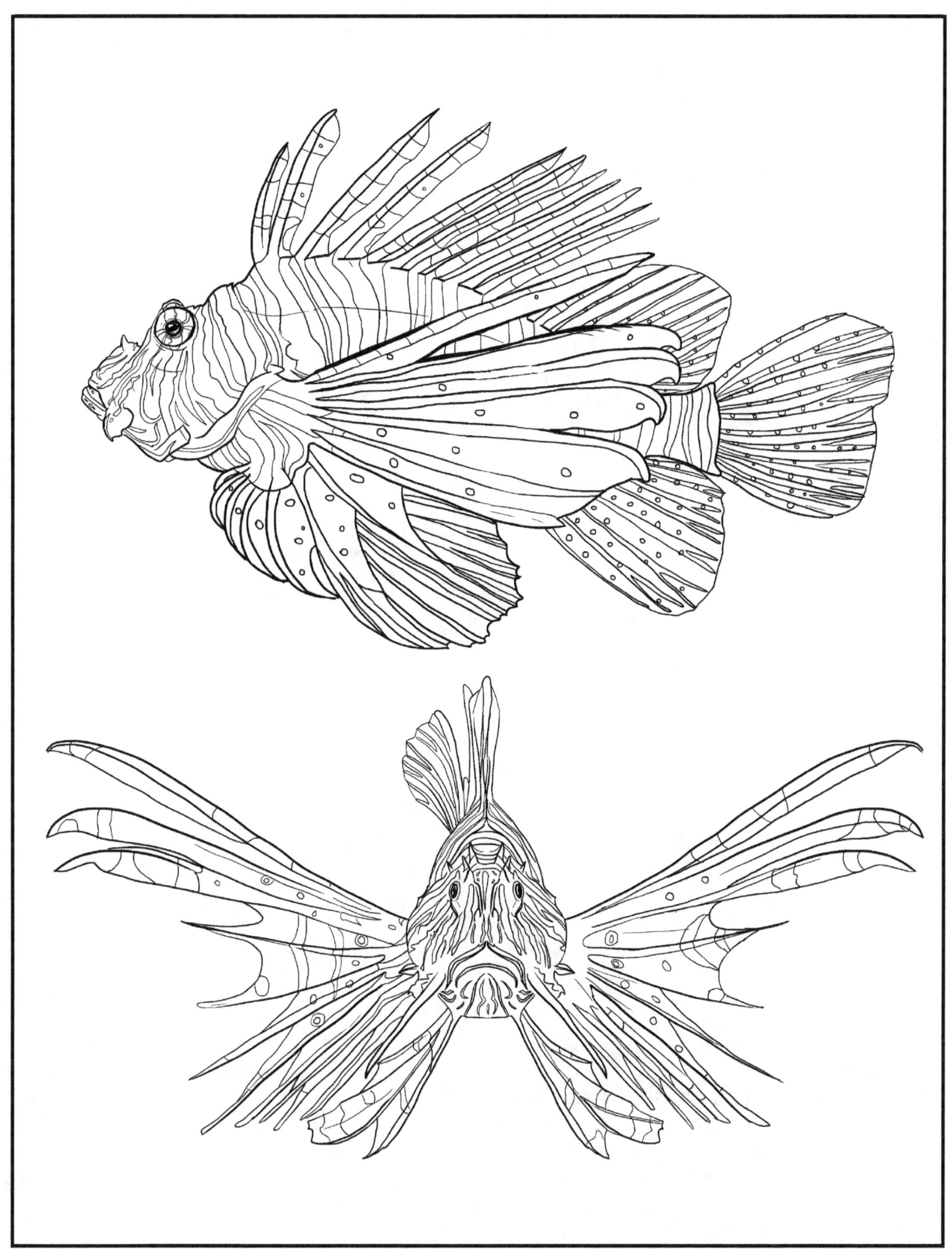

15. Lionfish
Animal species: red lionfish (Pterois volitans)

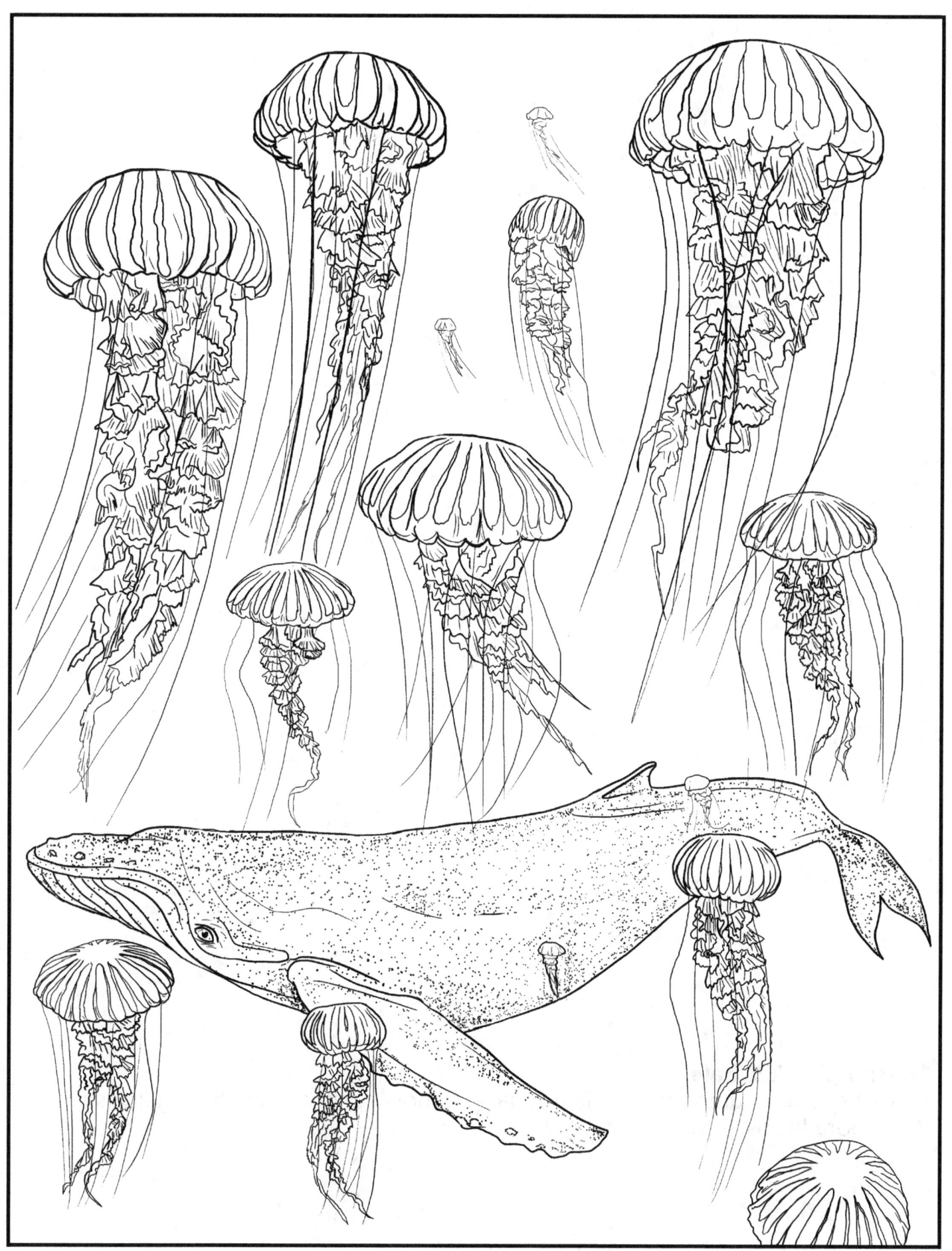

16. Humpback Whale
Animal species: humpback whale (Megaptera novaeangliae), compass jellyfish (Chrysaora hysoscella)

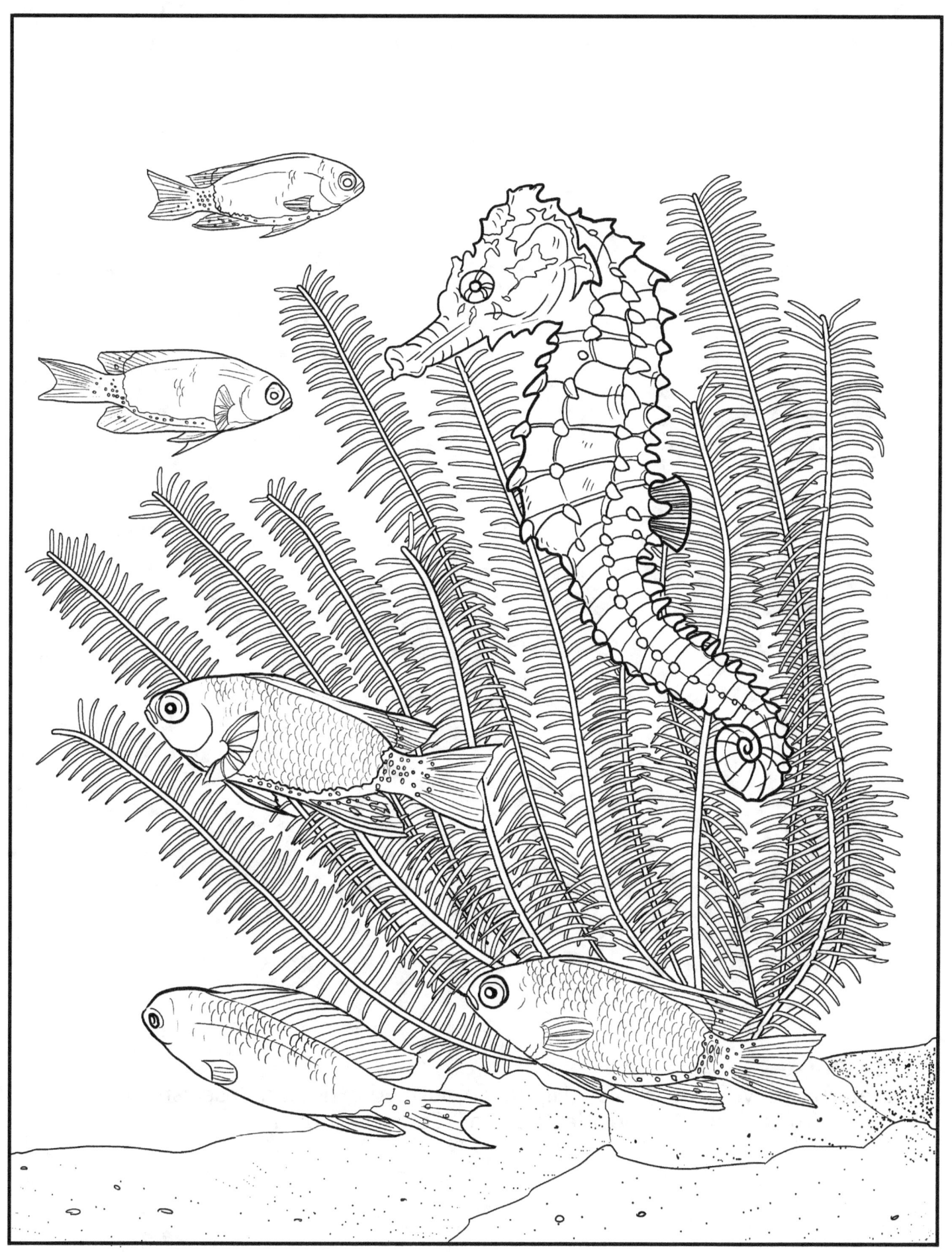

17. Seahorse
Animal species: yellow seahorse (Hippocampus kuda), neon damselfish (Pomacentrus coelestis), yellow feather star (Comaster nobilis)

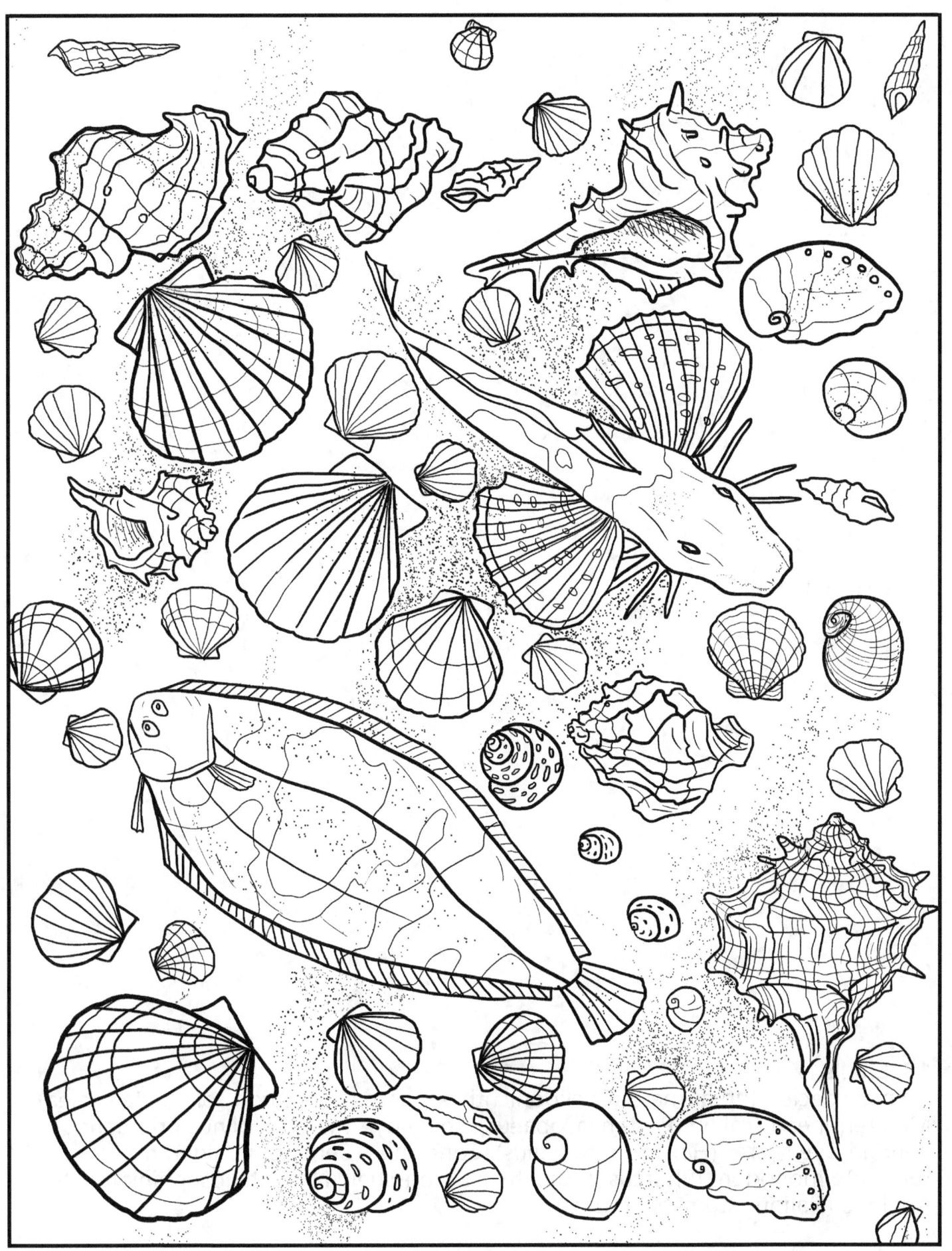

18. Shells
Animal species: tub gurnard (Chelidonichthys lucerna), common sole (Solea solea), Mediterranean scallop (Pecten jacobaeus), spiny dye-murex (Bolinus brandaris), Banded Dye Murex (Hexaplex trunculus), Cone shell (Cerithium vulgatum), turbinate monodont (Phorcus turbinatus), Moon-shell (Neverita josephinia), Abalone (Haliotis stomatiaeformis)

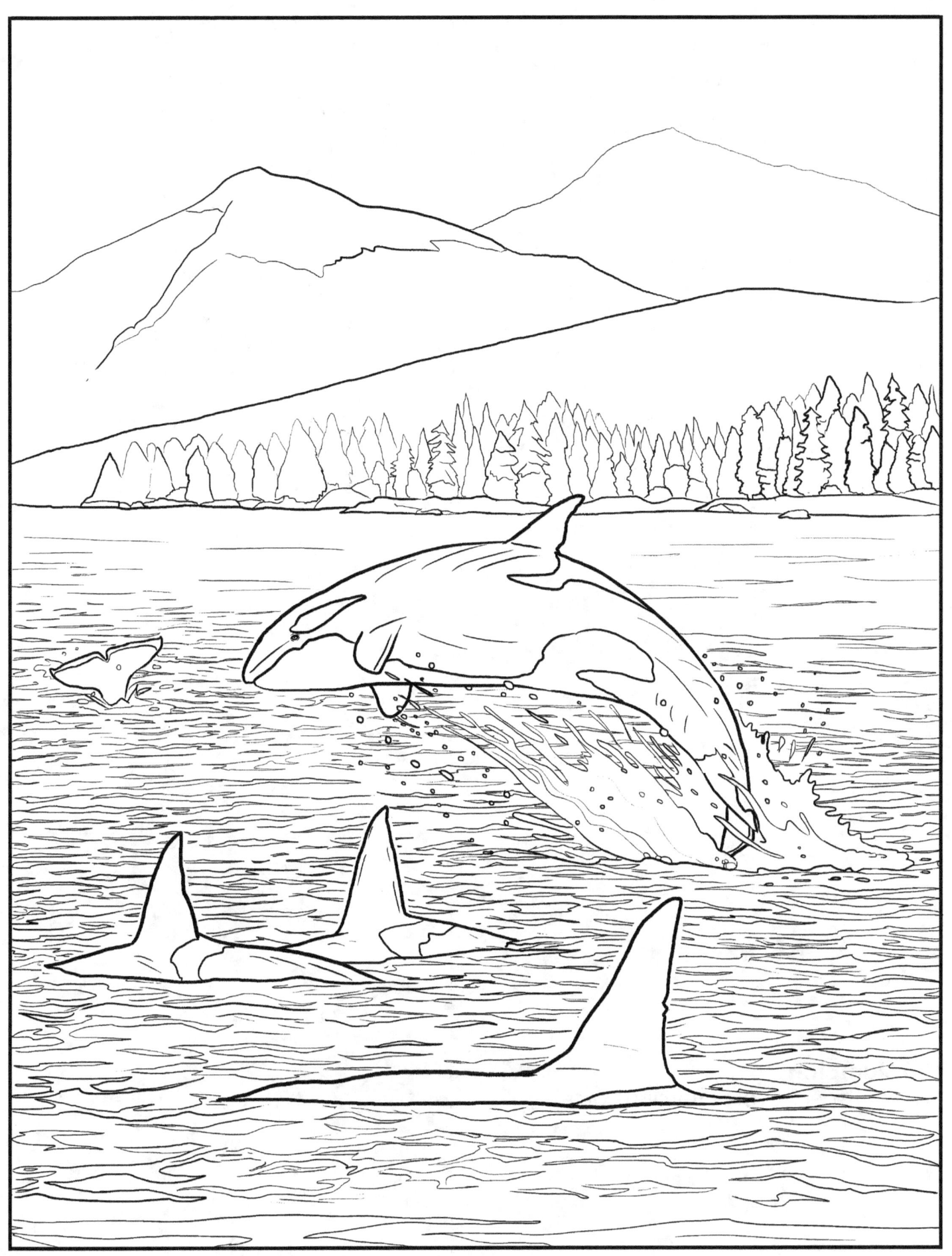

19. Jumping
Animal species: orca (Orcinus orca)

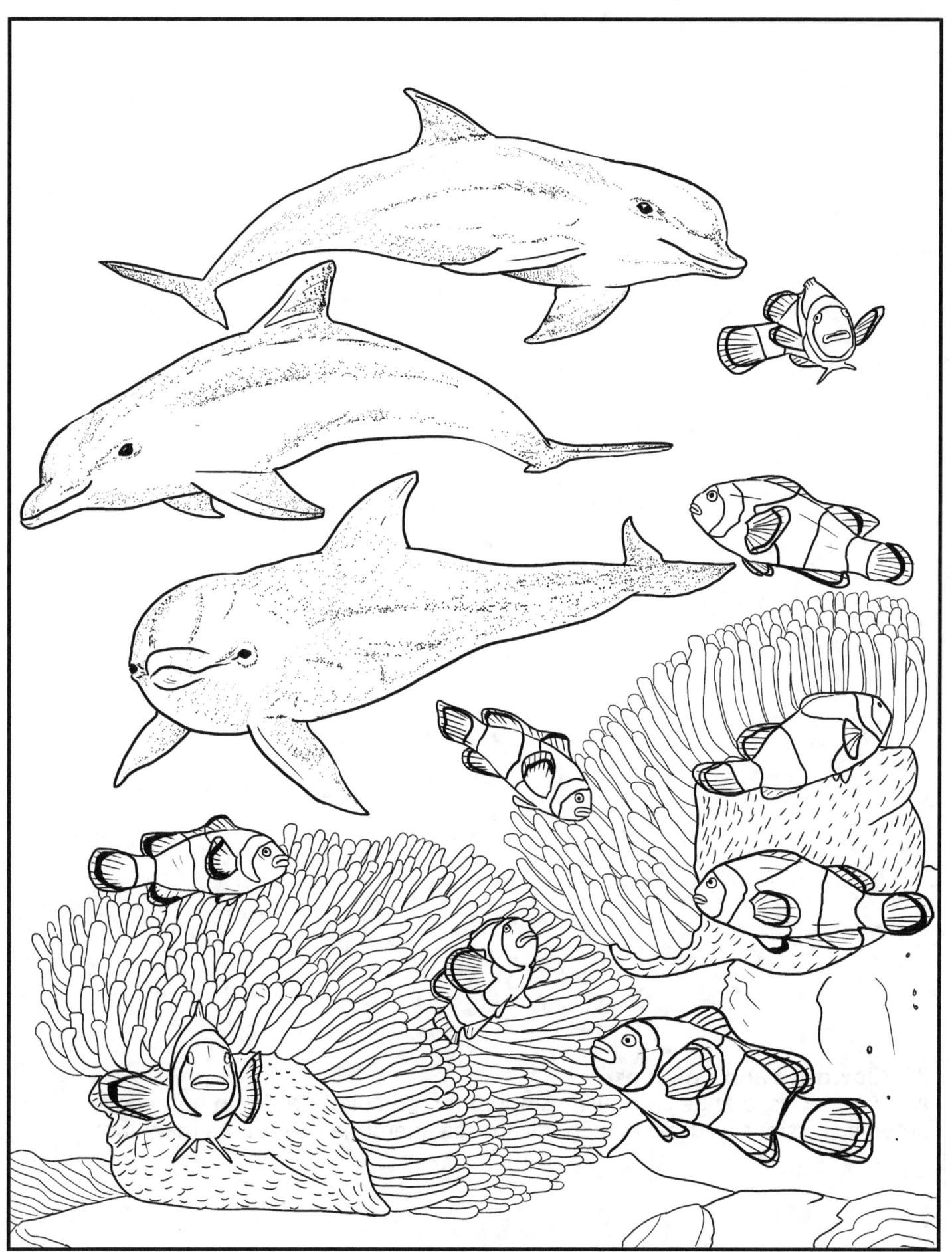

20. Clownfish and Dolphins
Animal species: orange clownfish (Amphiprion percula) , common bottlenose dolphin (Tursiops truncatus), magnificent sea anemone (Heteractis magnifica)

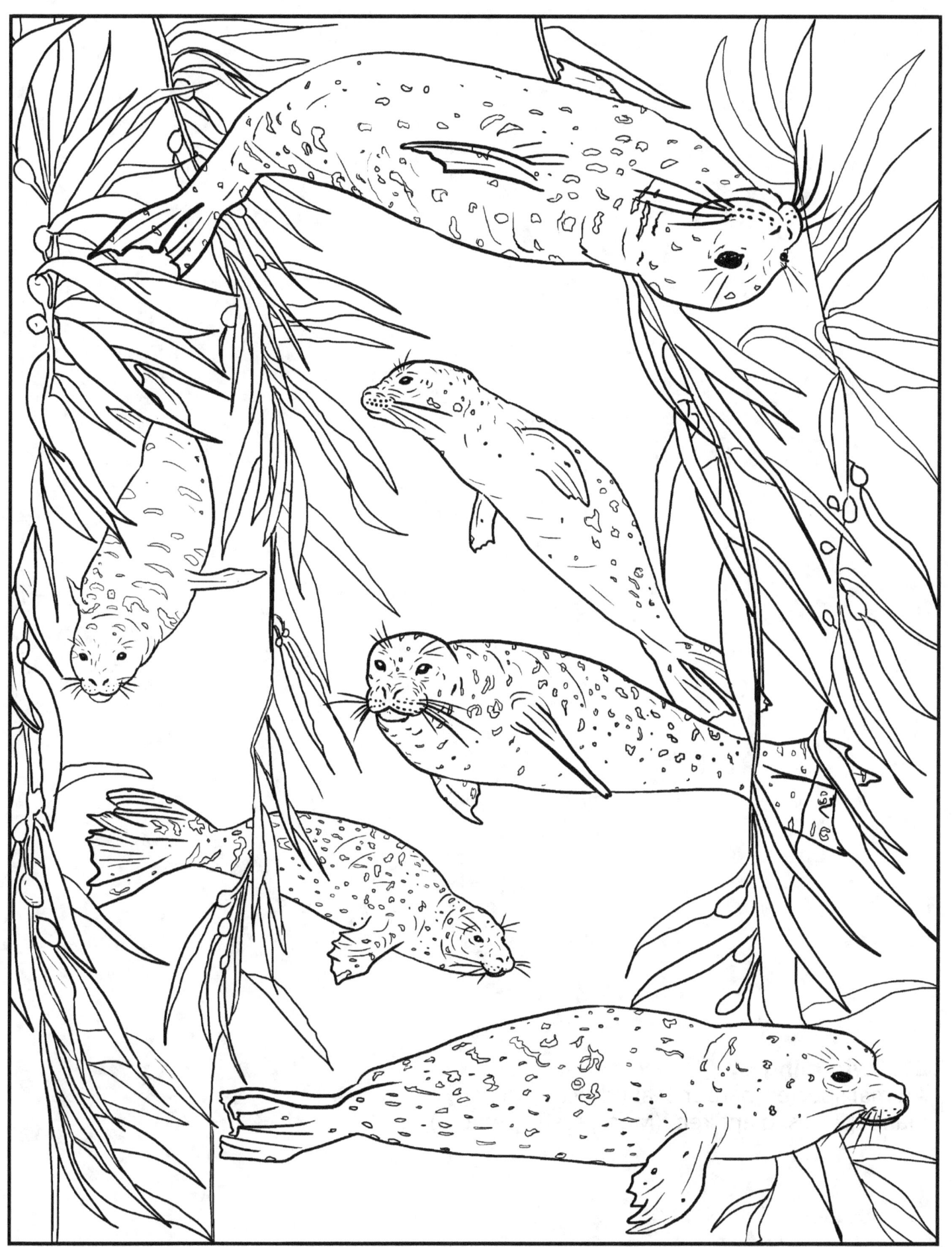

21. Swimming
Animal species: harbor seal (Phoca vitulina)
Plant species: giant kelp (Macrocystis pyrifera)

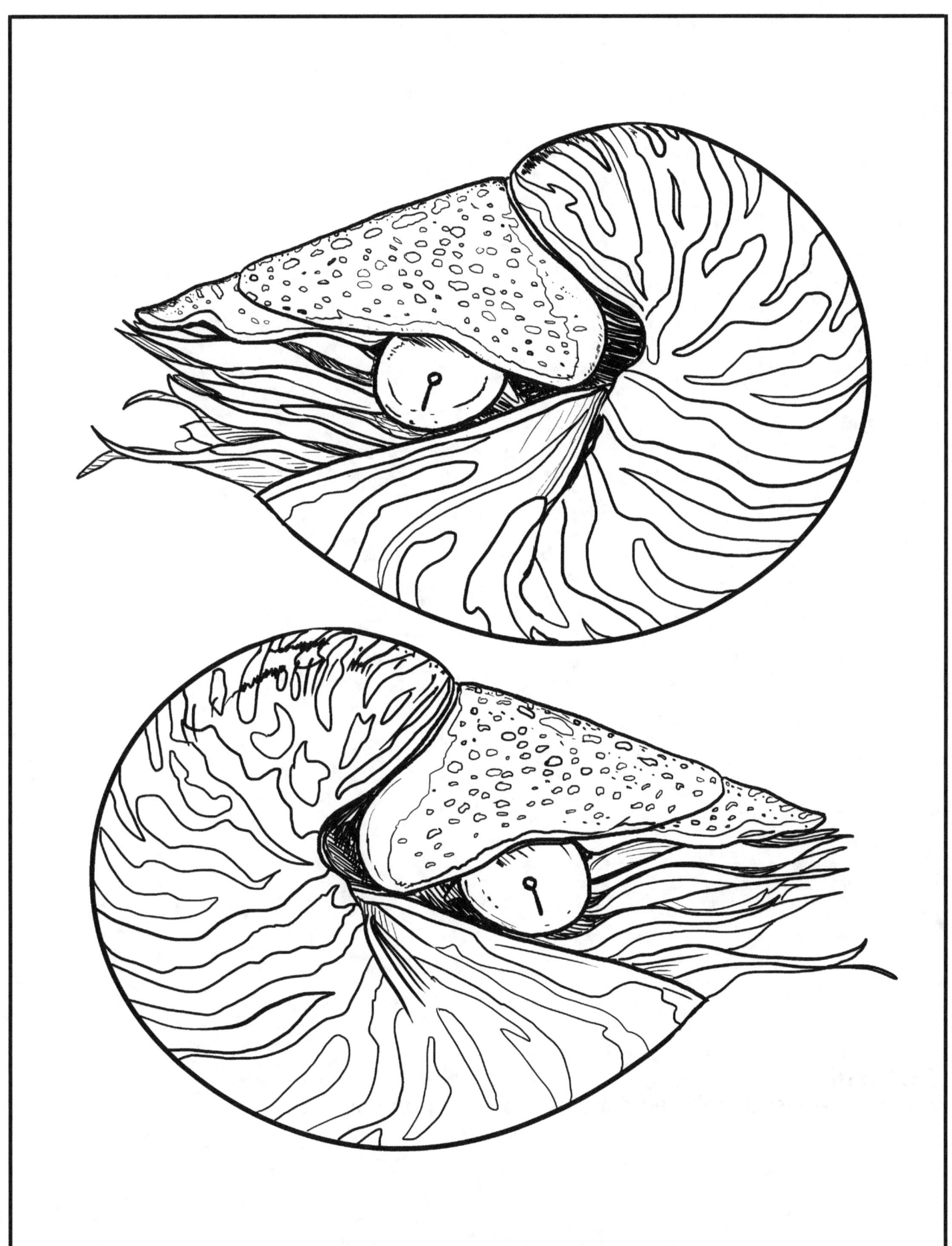

22. Nautilus
Animal species: chambered nautilus (Nautilus pompilius)

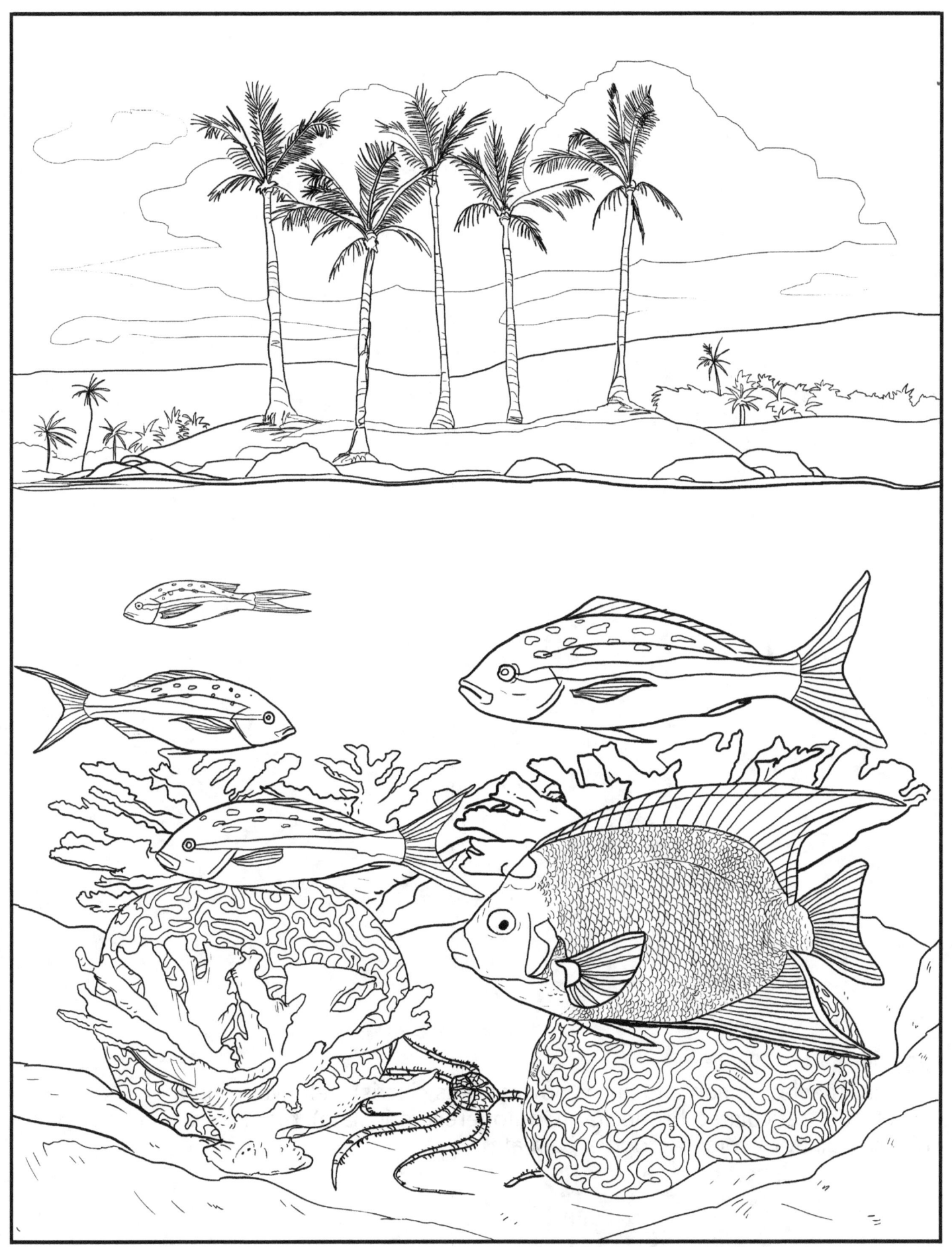

23. Palms
Animal species: queen angelfish (Holacanthus ciliaris), yellowtail snapper (Ocyurus chrysurus), reticulated brittle star (Ophionereis reticulata), brain coral (Colpophyllia natans), Elkhorn coral (Acropora palmata)

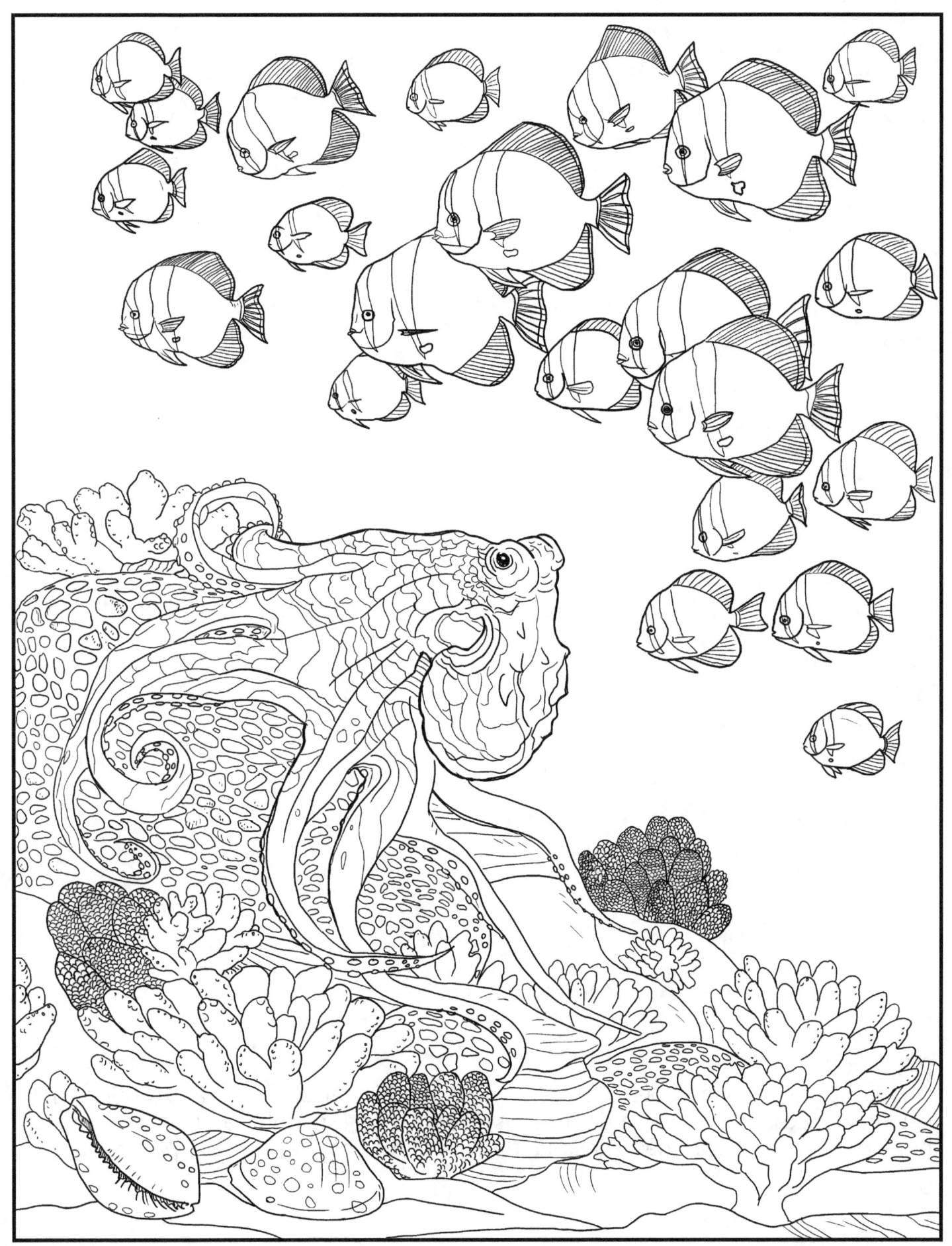

24. Red Sea
Animal species: day octopus (Octopus cyanea), orbicular batfish (Platax orbicularis), cauliflower coral (Pocillopora damicornis), hood coral (Stylophora pistillata), honeycomb coral (Gardineroseris planulata), panther cowry (Cypraea pantherina)

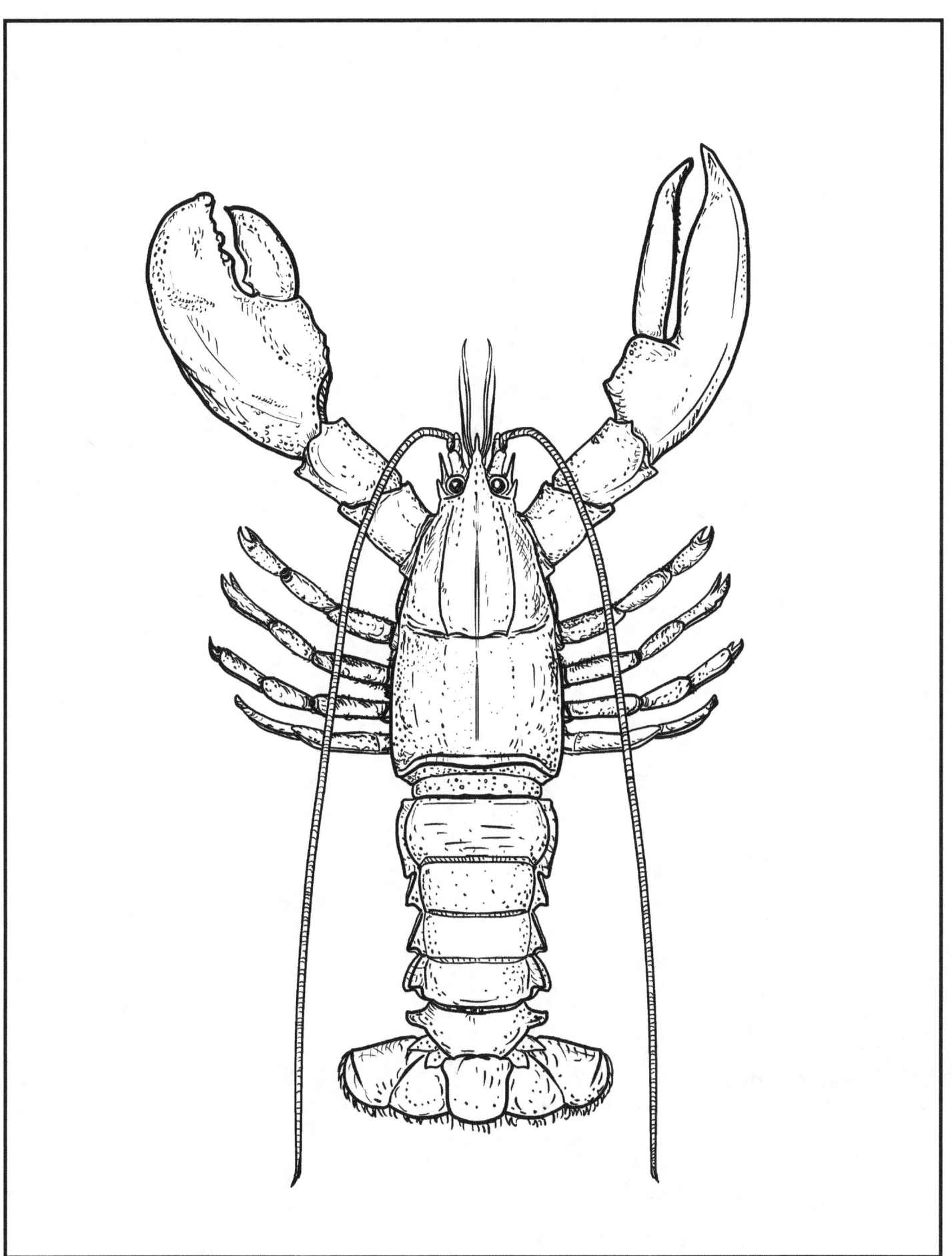

25. American lobster
Animal species: American lobster (Homarus americanus)

By the same author

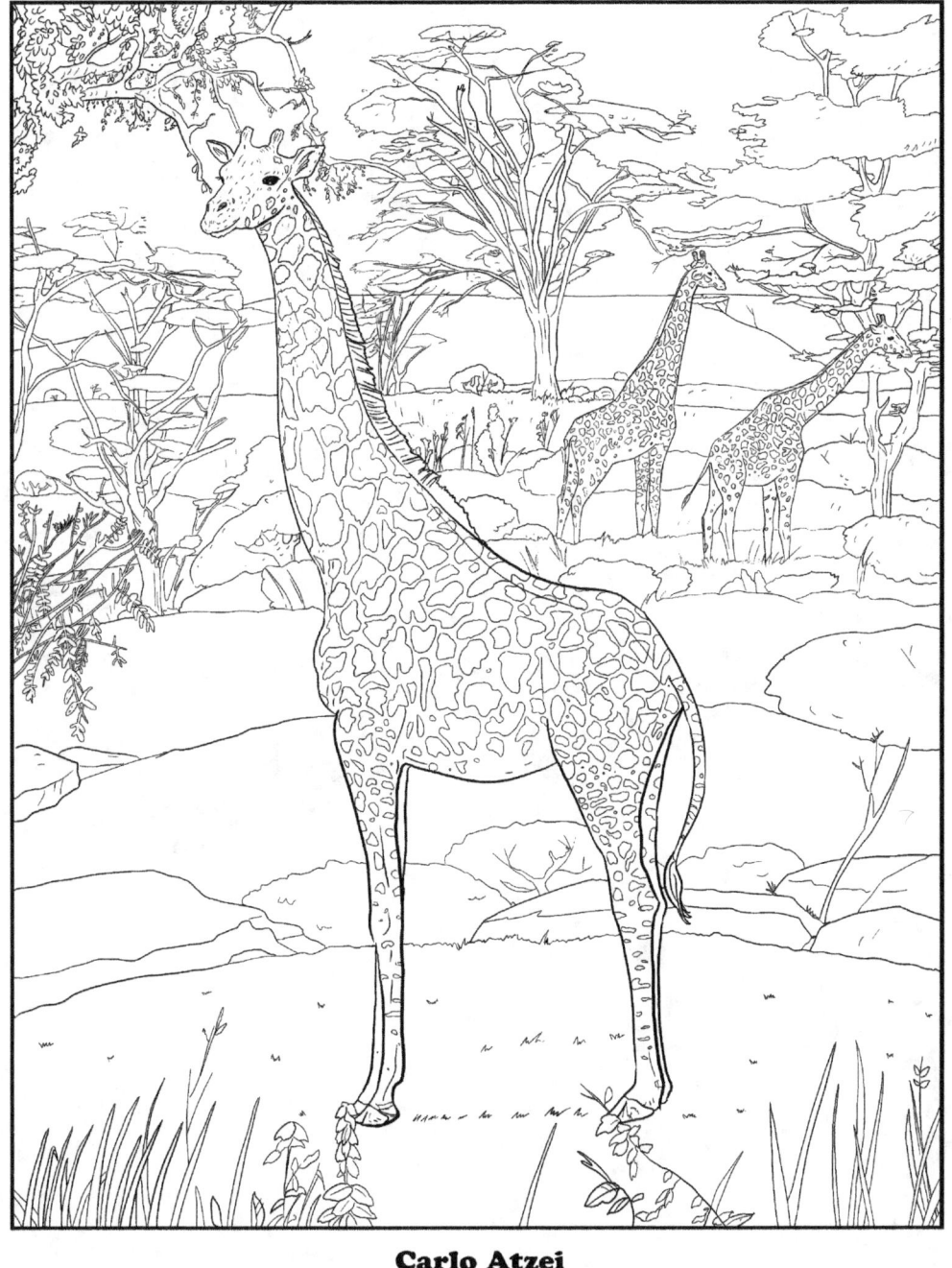

amazon.com/author/carloatzei

www.ingramcontent.com/pod-product-compliance
Lightning Source LLC
Chambersburg PA
CBHW080441220526
45465CB00007B/2726